In Splendid Detail

NEEDLEPOINT ART

CATHERINE REURS

TEXT BY JILL HERBERS

PHOTOGRAPHY BY RICHARD DESMARAIS

STEWART, TABORI & CHANG

NEW YORK

Title page: The "Bacchus" pillow portrays the god of wine in a boat under hanging grape vines on the Mediterranean Sea. This design was inspired by a piece of ancient Greek pottery, and the complicated stitching is intended to show the cracked terra-cotta as it looks today.

Contents page: The inspiration for the "Quimper" pillows came from a piece of French pottery. The design, which comes from the province of Brittany, has been used on pottery for over three hundred years.

Section openers: page 1, "Flying Fish" pillow; page 15, "Robb House" portrait; page 39, "Black-and-White Angels"; page 65, "Mondrian" pillow; page 93, box of knickknacks; page 125, "Earth" bag.

Text copyright © 1991 Catherine Reurs
Photographs copyright © 1991 Richard Desmarais
Photograph page 67 copyright © 1991 Jonathan Wallen

Published in 1991 by
Stewart, Tabori & Chang, Inc.
575 Broadway, New York, New York 10012

Library of Congress Cataloging-in-Publication Data

Reurs, Catherine.
In splendid detail : needlepoint art / by Catherine Reurs ; text by Jill Herbers : photography by Richard Desmarais.
        p.   cm.
ISBN 1-55670-185-3
1. Canvas embroidery. 2. Canvas embroidery—Patterns.
I. Herbers, Jill.   II. Title.
TT778.C3R44   1991
746.44'2—dc20
91-12766
CIP

All charts by Camilla Franklin of W. Yorkshire, England, using APSO © Cadet Software.

Distributed in the U.S. by Workman Publishing, 708 Broadway, New York, New York 10003
Distributed in Canada by Canadian Manda Group, P.O. Box 920 Station U, Toronto, Ontario M8Z 5P9
Distributed in all other territories by Little, Brown and Company, International Division, 34 Beacon Street, Boston, Massachusetts 02108

Printed in Singapore

10 9 8 7 6 5 4 3 2 1

In loving memory of my father,
John H. Reurs

∎

$\mathcal{C}$ontents

Introduction

■ ■ ■ ■ ■

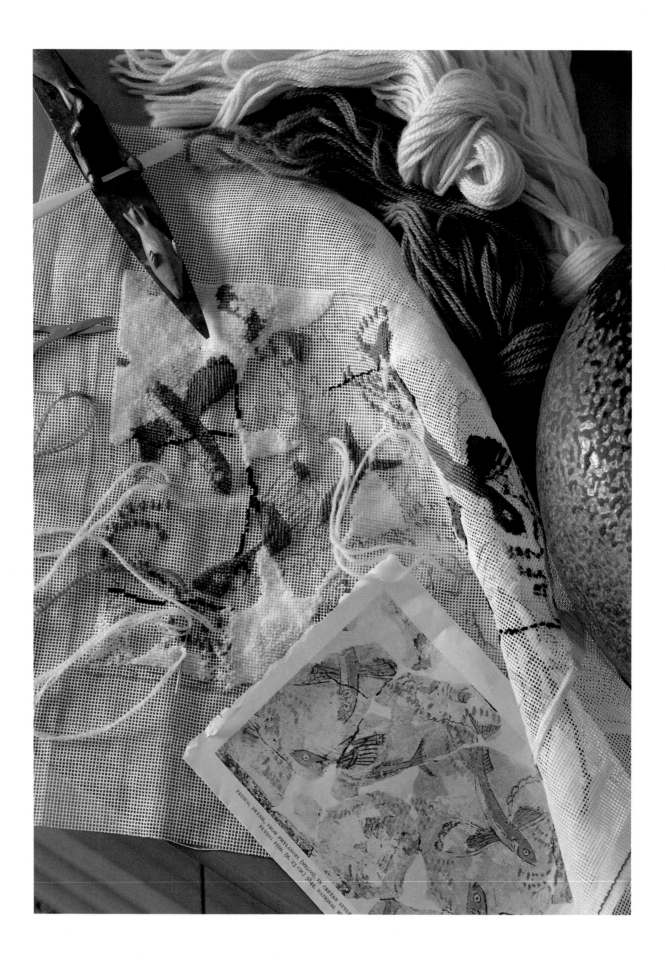

FRESCO DETAIL FROM PHYLAKOPI (MELOS) IN CRETAN STYLE
FLYING FISH (H. 23 CM.) 594, NATIONAL MU

Mention needlepoint, and all too often people think of a quaint hobby and prefabricated canvases with pictures of sweet flowers, puppies, and wide-eyed children. I like flowers, puppies, and children as much as the next person, but needlepoint is so much more. In truth, it has been a venerable art form for centuries, from the needle-point-upholstered sofas and chairs that sat in ancient palaces—and are now preserved in the best museums—to the intricately stitched items that adorned the intimate domains of historical figures like Mary, Queen of Scots and Queen Victoria.

In the last decade or so, artists like Kaffe Fassett have begun something of a revolution in the needlework field. With his bold and original designs, Fassett has successfully challenged the idea that knitting and needlepointing are dull, restrained, and limited to certain subjects or patterns. Of course, craftsmanship is central to needlework, but the freedom to use it in innovative ways and with infinite designs is what allows it to be raised from the level of craft to art.

Personally, I knew that needlepoint was much more than a craft when, as a teenager, I went to a store seeking my first canvas. Rather than work on one of the predesigned canvases for sale there—trite, happy faces, bland butterflies,

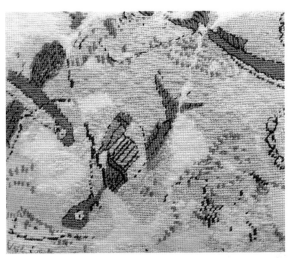

Left: This montage of the "Flying Fish" pillow includes a picture of the original Greek fresco, the inspiration for my design. Above: A detail of the pillow.

and somewhat hackneyed flower scenes—I asked the proprietress if it would be possible for me to make up my own design. She very kindly offered to sell me the blank canvas, but cautioned me to start on something small and not too complex. I took the canvas, but stubbornly refused her advice, launching on an intricate pattern inspired by three Oriental rugs that my grandparents, who collected antiques, kept in their home. The piece would take me three years to complete, but after that, I never really stopped stitching, through my somewhat unlikely career in the fast-paced world of banking to my full-time profession as a designer of original needlepoint creations.

■

By the time I became a second vice-president at Chase Manhattan Bank in Milan in 1984, needlepoint had become a necessary antidote to stress. Because it is so portable, I was able to design and stitch my own pieces while travelling throughout Europe on business: on airplanes, where I spent much of my time; in hotel rooms after the business day was over; and while riding the subway in London. It gave me great satisfaction to look into my briefcase and see a needlepoint canvas and the vibrant colors of Persian wool alongside my official bank documents.

Slowly, as friends became aware of my designs, they began to commission works for their own homes, and my revered pastime became a small side-business. When the stock market crashed in 1987 and my entire department was laid off, fate took its course and I proceeded to turn my side-business into a full-time profession. It may seem like a big leap—from wearing wool suits to stitching wool—but, given my upbringing, it really is not so strange. As is

common in the United States, my ancestors came from many different countries, which meant that I was always surrounded by international influences. Furthermore, I grew up amid the Oriental rugs, Belgian lace, and other textiles that my grandparents collected. I earned a degree in art history in college, and remained interested in the arts—even when I was entrenched in the business world. Like many of us, I took a roundabout route to my true calling.

THE DECORATIVE ARTS REVISITED

More than ever, the home has become a refuge from the world, where people can express themselves—personally and individually. A stenciled floor or handwoven rug can provide a sense of intimacy that no amount of merchandise from a department store can achieve. No matter how unique a contemporary home is, there is bound to be a computer on the desk, a microwave in the kitchen, and machine-made furniture and objects throughout. The textures, lines, and character of decorative arts—be they centuries-old paintings, ceramics, or needlework—relieve that lack of humanism and give a room the feeling that human hands have shaped what is there. The decorative arts serve to soften the landscape of high-tech objects that inevitably makes up so much of our living space today.

A client once came to my house to commission a pillow after she had seen one of my designs pictured in a magazine. When she asked if it would be possible to see the original, I told her that I believed she was sitting on it. She seemed alarmed—and then charmed—that something so pristinely pictured in a glossy magazine could be so accessible.

It is most striking that even an art as old as needlepoint

can be woven into modern settings, and both the needlework and the interiors benefit. Very contemporary designs
can be applied to the canvas, such as the *Mondrian* pillows
pictured in the last chapter of this book (page 86). Or
ancient influences, such as the tiger rugs of Tiber, can be
reinterpreted in a contemporary vein. (My version of a tiger
rug can be found in the last chapter.) Perhaps most important, though, is the fact that even pieces with very traditional designs can work in both period and contemporary
interiors. To the surprise and delight of many, a needlepoint
pillow can be as compelling on a Biedermeier sofa as on a
Barcelona chair or a Frank Lloyd Wright bench. In this
book, some pieces are shown in both contemporary and
traditional settings to demonstrate how successfully they
can be incorporated into both worlds.

When I design needlepoint creations, I approach them as an
artist would a canvas. Nothing has to go in a particular
place; an infinite variety of shapes and forms are possible.
And unlike knitting, where one starts at one end
of the piece and works to the other, I can begin
anywhere on the canvas and move around as I
see fit, which makes it like painting with wool.
This is not to say that I limit my materials to
wool. I will unhesitatingly use whatever en-
hances the piece, including thread, beads, and
trim. Once I even used wheat to surround a
needlepoint picture of a field (page 44). On another occasion I "gilded" the border of a pillow with gold
coins (page 52). This free approach to the canvas is a departure from tradition, but needlepoint creations can be made
even more adventurous by exploring different subjects and

PAINTING
WITH WOOL

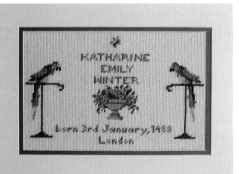

*Following pages: Flags
needlepointed in miniature
bring the imposing symbols
down to a more personal
level, allowing us to
appreciate them not only
for their patriotic messages
but for their distinctive
designs as well.*

influences. Anything that intrigues me could end up in my work—petroglyphs from rock outcroppings on a chair seat, African designs on a chessboard, patterns from Italian pottery on a pillow, or free-form designs picked up from old fish decoys on a contemporary piece. Design ideas and variations can be taken from the wallpaper in the living room, the flowers in the garden, or a simple Shaker pattern spotted in an antique shop.

I am fascinated by the colors, patterns, and vibrancy of the designs of cultures that are foreign to me. African, Indian, Guatemalan, Mayan, Mexican, and American-Indian influences are such a departure from the more re-

strained European and American designs I grew up with that they seem wholly new and fresh to me. When I borrow these influences, I do not try to create a design that echoes one particular culture, but instead try to combine subjects, colors, tones, and uses from a variety of different areas with the goal of creating something unique. For example, I covered a pair of plain bedroom slippers in a Guatemalan splash of colors (page 91), and I combined influences from India and American folk art to create the *Zig-Zag* footstool (page 81). This mixing of previously unrelated influences allows for an infinite diversity of expression—a technique that I do not believe has been explored nearly enough in the field of needlepoint.

SUBTLETY OF COLOR

As the granddaughter of antique collectors, the world at my feet was often made up of fine Oriental rugs. Thus I learned very early that these rugs are not merely color and pattern but are actually a great mix of colors: for every rug with navy-blue in it, there may be twenty-five shades of the color; whites may appear in dozens of different tones; there are varying degrees of fading and vibrancy. The resulting subtlety is part of what elevates Oriental rugs from the category of craft to the more esteemed classification of works of art, and it is what gives them character and texture, richness and depth.

I take the same approach with needlepoint, sometimes using dozens of shades of one color to create that same sense of light and shadow, that complexity of blending and shading. In the *Flying Fish* pillow (see detail page 3), for instance, I used sixteen tones of white. In this way, I think some of my canvases resemble impressionist paintings. I create not just a scene but a mood.

But if these varying tones and shades lend a sense of the artistic to Oriental rugs, they are also what imbue the rugs with a human element, and make one aware that they were lived with and were a part of people's lives, as much while they were being made as after they were laid on the floor. For unlike my approach, the use of so many different colors was not intentional on the part of the nomadic tribes that originally created the rugs. Because they travelled so much, they brought with them only the most valued items, which included their rugs in progress and their sheep, but did not include enough dyed wool for an entire rug. Instead, when the wool they were carrying ran out, they would shear their sheep and have a certain amount of the wool dyed, but, again, not enough to complete the rug. By the time their wool ran out again, the tribe was inevitably in a different town, and though each

An ancient Japanese tradition inspired me to create this industrial-style doorstop. In some areas of Japan, when a couple is married, a rope is tied around two protruding rocks off the coast of Japan, symbolizing the couple's union. In a similar way, this concrete-block doorstop is tied up with heavy purple cord.

new batch of wool was meant to be the same navy or red or green as the last batch, it was dyed by hand in an inexact process, and it never came out quite the same color. In fact, if you look closely at older rugs, you can even see where one shade stops and another starts, marking the shearing of sheep and the tribe's arrival in another town.

This page: As this regal bear demonstrates, whimsy has its place in the decorative arts. This Napoleon hat was designed expressly for him. Right: Lots of midnight blues and purples were used behind these polar bears to represent the aurora borealis. The hearts add warmth to the cool colors, and the shiny black beads give the bears' eyes extra sparkle.

I've drawn on this heritage to give a complexity to my pieces, making them more narrative and broad and, in some cases, more realistic since the eye picks up many different colors to perceive just a few. Also parallel to my vision of needlepoint is the idea that the people of these tribes lived with their rugs constantly: so it is for all of us who devote the many hours required to complete a well-loved canvas.

1

European and Classical Traditions

The decorative traditions of Europe are rich and complex, offering much for the modern-day artist to draw upon. But, unlike the decorative arts of the New World, where personal inspiration and tradition guided the artist, the arts of Europe were, for centuries, directed by an aristocratic system and the church. The pieces in this chapter hark back to these grand traditions as well as to the equally inspiring classical traditions of ancient Greece, Rome, Egypt, and even Turkey, all of which had strong influences on European design.

From traditional French and Italian pottery I derived the designs for the *Orvieto* and *Quimper* pillows. These patterns have been used for centuries in small villages all over France and Italy, and it is clear that their endurance is due to the purity and simplicity of their design. It is from tapestries in the Cluny Museum in Paris that I found the design for the *Medieval Bunny* pillow. Traditional Scandinavian sweaters served as inspiration for the *Noah's Ark* pillow in which biblical animals replace snowflakes and trees as the primary design motif.

The house portraits in this chapter are all from England, with a variety of country houses, town houses, and grand buildings. For each portrait, I used a snapshot of the building as a guide and transferred the lines and shapes of the

Left: A group of friends commissioned this portrait of the "Kensington House" for a woman who was leaving London for America. Above: Though cherubs are traditional mascots of Victorian design, this pair works well in a contemporary setting.

E U R O P E A N

architecture and its surroundings to the canvas. I stitched in as much detail as I could, sometimes using layers of thread to create a three-dimensional effect for, say, window boxes, lawns, or brick paths.

The portrait of the renowned Palm Court in the Ritz Hotel in London is the most difficult project I have ever undertaken. The decor is so ornate that to show the detail I wanted, I had to use a very small mesh canvas—eighteen stitches to the inch. To capture the true effect of its intricate gilding, I used fifteen colors of gold thread—pink gold, green gold, and purple gold, for example. As with all my pieces, if a particular section didn't come out as I liked, I took out the stitches and tried something new. After 31,000 stitches and 150 hours, I finally finished it.

For the pieces based on classical themes in this chapter I relied on drawings and photos of murals, ancient pottery, and wall-hangings. Two of the pieces—the *Flying Fish* pillow and the *Bacchus* pillow—both inspired by ancient Greek designs, were designed to work with a client's Beidermeier furniture, which is based on Greek lines and forms. The *Flying Fish* pillow was inspired by a mural that had been cracked and repaired many times. To get a mottled effect, I used over a dozen shades of white thread—the whitest representing the part of the mural that was repaired most recently with plaster. The design of the *Bacchus* pillow was taken from a piece of pottery that complemented the yellow and black tones of Beidermeier furniture. It, too, had cracks that I tried to incorporate into my design. These were especially challenging pieces because I was not only trying to translate the texture and lines of one medium—in this case pottery and a mural—to another, but I was also trying to make something new look old. Other classical pieces include the *Roman Temple* clock, actually an unfinished pine

A friend's antique shop in London made a perfect subject for a portrait. I tried to catch every detail—from the flecked stone of the building to the antiques displayed in the shop window.

clock kit on which I needlepointed rather than painted the face, and the *Papyrus Flowers* pillow that is based on the stylized designs of ancient Egypt.

The pieces in this chapter take a sweeping look at many cultures and many times. Although meant to reflect histori-

cal traditions, they can take on a contemporary feel when interpreted through modern eyes. This chapter contains my own ideas about how this subtle transformation—from old to new—can be achieved. However, everyone has a different vision, and the infinite variety of creations that results is what makes designing needlepoint such a fascinating personal adventure.

Above: The Golfar House is part of a row of typically English townhouses in the Pimlico section of London. It took a lot of color mixing to show the house's age and the variations in its bricks. Right: A wooden playhorse on wheels is the centerpiece for a nontraditional birth announcement.

The Palm Court at the heart of the Ritz
inspired by the celebrated fountain known as

LONDON   RITZ

Purple gold, green gold, yellow gold, and a dozen other shades of gilded thread, along with beads, sparkles, and layer upon layer of needlework were used to convey the glamour and glitz of the Palm Court in London's Ritz Hotel. Since there are several types of lighting in the complex room, choosing just the right shades of wool proved challenging. The colors looked different in every photograph I took, so I finally decided to visit the room with an assortment of wool in hand and match the colors on the spot. This was my most challenging portrait. To achieve the proper detail, I stitched on very fine mesh, which required a lot of stitches — 31,000 to be exact.

*Left: Tapestries from the Cluny Museum in Paris inspired the
"Medieval Bunny" pillow. The rope trim serves as an elegant "frame."
Above: St. Bride's Cottage sits by the sea in Wales. Amazingly, the
house really is as pink as it looks in the portrait.*

Left: In the "Goose with the Golden Egg," I used many shades of blue to capture the richness of the night sky, and varying shades of green to show the shadows of the geese created by the light of the moon above. Above: This cherub is based on a pattern I found in a turn-of-the-century copy of the Ladies Home Journal. *The couple who commissioned it for their Victorian house wanted the blue background of this piece to match the ceramic wall tiles in their home.*

*I*n this piece, inspired by a
Byzantine icon, I relied as
much on the frame as on
the subject to convey the
sense of mystery and richness central to the culture
and religion of Turkey.
This design came from a
fresco of a bishop in an
early Istanbul church.
A small mesh allowed me
to capture the detail of
the original art.

Formerly, when two people were married in Europe, their family crests were combined, which resulted in a whole new crest design. This is my grandparents' crest. The inscription reads, in Dutch, "May Courage Never Leave You."

*From the town of Orvieto in Italy came the centuries-old pottery
that inspired the design for this pillow, which looks as lovely on
the formally striped chair as on this spare contemporary sofa.
Following pages: Both beautiful and useful, the quintessentially
Victorian "Heart" pincushion takes a central place on a lady's dresser.*

*Needlepoint birth
announcements are
traditional in England.
In this case, the parents
held a special affection
for parrots.*

2

North American Influences

When I returned to the United States after living in Europe for many years, I looked at the folk art of North America in a new light. I saw the allure of American Victorian motifs and the charm of naive paintings and country scenes. I began to appreciate as never before how the early Americans, although obviously influenced by Old World traditions, were able to escape from the formality and mannered styles of European art to create an art that was a more honest interpretation of their everyday lives. To reflect the new freedom of the New World, I have used beads that sparkle, trim that dazzles, and dozens of different shades of wool to convey the light and shadow of an afternoon or the different tones of the night sky.

It is from that folk-art tradition that the pieces in this chapter were born. There are influences from the quilts that lay on old four-poster beds, from the embroidered alphabet samplers of early-American children, from the folk-art painting and furniture that is being created today, and from artists like Jasper Johns who recreated the American flag in his own unique fashion. Angels, a traditional folk symbol, appear throughout this chapter. There are portraits of the wilderness, of the rolling fields outside my window, and of real people's houses. There is even a watermelon piece,

Above: A heart in hand was a cherished Victorian love token. The repetition of hands marching across this pillow creates a more contemporary look. Left: The angled view of this house in Babylon, Long Island, makes this portrait different from most of my others.

A M E R I C A N

offering a literal slice of American life.

As in most of my work, I did not set out with strict artistic goals when I began to create these pieces. I simply kept my mind open to the influences that surrounded me. I decided to make the *Watermelon* eyeglass case when I caught sight of a bright green zipper, which reminded me of a watermelon rind, on an unimpressive argyle eyeglass case in a needle-point store. I immediately bought a real watermelon and matched the abstract natural patterns on the rind and the vibrant reds of the fruit to the wool before eating the model! In the *Pendleton* stool cover, I was inspired by the traditions of the Southwest, particularly the antique Pendleton blankets

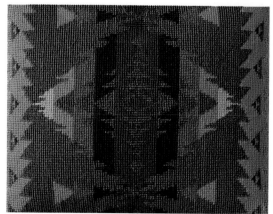

that imitate ancient Navajo designs. In the *Navajo* pillow, I again echoed those Native American themes. I added a new dimension to this project by using faded yarn to achieve the "dusty" look of the Old West and to give the piece the feel of something that is old and well worn.

In a very different vein, I also used Victorian themes in many of the pieces in this chapter. For inspiration, I looked through old books of Victorian valentine patterns and ladies' magazines from the 1890s. I didn't allow the rigidity of Victorian culture to put constraints on my imagination as I trimmed the *Angel* pincushion with gold coins after reading that Indians sewed shells all around their pillows for ornamentation. This is a good example of how I mix ideas from different cultures in the same piece. Again, unimpeded by tradition, I often choose unorthodox forms like the dalmation for my needlepoint Christmas ornaments. I like to use very sparkly thread and trim on these ornaments so they will not get lost in my tree. Glitter allows the Christmas lights to pick up their color and form.

I rescued the "Pendleton" stool from an antique shop, where it sat sadly covered in polyester. A Pendleton blanket provided the rich patterns and colors that completely transformed this cushion design.

Although my house portraits appear throughout this book because of their varying architectural styles, the buildings in this chapter are all either American or Canadian. Interestingly, these portraits, which constitute a great deal of my work, began quite by accident. My mother requested a needlepoint picture of her house for Christmas and, al-

This page: The "Wheatfields" mirror is one of a series of mirror frames I have made in needlepoint. The exotic wheat trim amplifies the rolling fields that I needlepointed in abstract forms to convey a sense of land and sky in shadow and light.
Right: My father's lovely Connecticut farmhouse is surrounded by huge old sycamore and maple trees. I did the leaves last, on top of the base stitching, to give the trees a three-dimensional effect.

though it had never occurred to me to undertake such a project, I said I would try. Houses lend themselves very well to this medium and the result was much better than I had expected. After completing my mother's house portrait, I made one of my father's house, and the portraits took off from there with commissions and requests resulting in nearly two dozen portraits to date.

Left: This egg cozy is a small tribute to the Canadian flag. Pieces like this one are wonderful for beginners because they can be finished in a matter of hours. Above: Sometimes measuring by eye can be risky. When I made this tea cozy, I slightly underestimated how much space all those stars would take up. To compensate, the top stripe had to be fatter than the others, and the top row of stars is indicated by a row of small dots. I think it is those idiosyncrasies that make the piece more personal and interesting.

Actress and model Isabella Rossellini sent me a photograph of her house on Long Island for a needlepoint portrait. I tried to capture the light and shade that blankets it on a summer's day. To achieve this effect, I deepened the shade of the colors as I stitched toward the right side of the piece. This little studio, which is behind the main house, is where she goes to be alone, and my portrait is meant to convey that privacy and intimacy.

*A*bove: *The Shaw House in Ottawa, Canada, is a townhouse
that looks so different from the back and front that one could
believe it to be two separate structures. While the front is formal
brick, the back is lovely weathered cedar. Right: Wild animals roam
across this folksy pillow. Changing the background color to, say,
blue, yellow, or green, would create a completely different effect.*

The "Angel" pincushion was inspired by folk-art Christmas ornaments that I saw in a New England antique shop. Since the angel is a revered folk symbol, I decided to cover and surround this one in gold—with gold thread for the wings, sequins for the stars, and a treasure of coins framing her. *Following pages, left:* That classic American symbol, the watermelon, makes for a humorous design on an eyeglass case. The back of the case displays the intriguing natural patterns of a watermelon rind, while the black seeds jump out of the magenta-colored fruit on the front. *Right:* The drapery of trees adds to the appeal of this lovely turn-of-the-century house in Pennsylvania.

BLANKET, brief style
A. 5141-6
128.0

Left: To replicate both the age and dust of the Old West, I mixed charcoal gray and navy blue with vibrant Navajo colors. Below: The "Navajo" pillow was inspired by a Native American rug design and is shown here on dollhouse furniture. These miniature pieces are reminiscent of those made by journey-men in England when they were learning to make dovetail joints.

Above: Dogs are beloved folk-art subjects. The portrait is of Bertie, a favorite family dog. The pillow features a Labrador; I placed him on a plain green background to achieve a classic simplicity of design. Right: My first house portrait of my mother's house in Massachusetts has a particularly naïve feel to it. While there are other buildings and trees abutting the house, I chose to leave them out and focus attention on the house itself.

Hummingbirds hover as they prepare to feed on nectar from their favorite flower—the Bergamot. I also created this pillow with a dark green background (shown on the cover), a more dramatic approach to the same design..

*A*bove: *A Dalmatian, a silver-maned horse, a pineapple, and a Japanese fan are fun departures from traditional Christmas ornaments. The argyle diamond and the striped heart make for less adventuresome but equally attractive decorations. Bright colors and sparkly materials keep the ornaments from getting lost in the tree. Right: Creating this doll's-house rug gave me the opportunity to design a rug without having to spend the hundreds of hours it takes to complete a full-size one. It was a refreshing break from tradition to stitch the camels in such a variety of colors.*

3

Contemporary Designs

■ ■ ■ ■ ■

Contemporary designs have rarely been explored in needle-point, perhaps because the craft is so often considered an old-fashioned one. When contemporary ideas are applied to this age-old art, the results can create a look that is exciting and fresh, as you will see in this chapter. These pieces are my most direct challenge to the established idea of needlepoint.

There are many ways in which a needlepoint piece may be considered contemporary. Some, like the *Mondrian* pillows, are influenced directly by modern art. Others, such as the *Petroglyph* chair-seat and *Tiger* rug, use ancient themes but in a free-form, abstract way. In the case of the Oriental rug pillows, the seemingly traditional designs from which I took my inspiration prove, upon close examination, to be quite abstract in their own right. In fact, the religion of the people who created these rugs did not allow graven images or literal representations in their designs, so they were forced to create abstract patterns.

In some cases, contemporary means working with a sense of humor, as in the *Purple Gallinules* pillow, which shows the absurd-looking gallinule birds in a stiffly formal pose. Even more humorous are the balloon chairs that I upholstered with wild petroglyphs: the chairs once served to accommodate the huge bustles of Victorian ladies and the

Left: The colors and stripes in this rug are evocative of real tiger skin. Above: Artist Don Johnson created the abstract design in the cushion of this stool which is the work of Dakota Jackson, a well-known furniture designer.

C O N T E M P O R A R Y

petroglyphs are symbols of a centuries-old Canadian Indian tribe. Although the Victorian era came over a thousand years after the Indians, I think this unexpected combination of styles works well together.

Contemporary pieces are fascinating to me, but it is when

The patterns for the "Ghana" chessboard came from a book of African textiles. African prints provide wonderful inspiration because they are bold, bright, and very graphic.

they are placed in surprising settings that they become most intriguing. I first realized this complementary relationship when I set two delicately colored *Rose* pillows, which I had made to match an Oriental rug, against a severely shaped modern Barcelona chair. Not only did the pillows soften its edges, but its starkness and simplicity showcased the needlepoint in a unique way that traditional overstuffed chairs and woven carpets could not. Once I knew that a suitably designed work could sit comfortably on a Frank Lloyd Wright bench or le Corbusier chair, I began using the

pillows based on Oriental rugs in contemporary interiors. I also began to experiment with the reverse by placing bold contemporary needlepoint designs among antique furnishings in traditional surroundings. But, in either case, combinations of traditional and contemporary cannot just be

thrown together. They need to be tied together by color, style, and form. Contrast can work beautifully, but only if it is done with the proper regard toward the pieces and their surroundings. In some cases all it takes is a certain trim to make a piece fit in with the rest of the room. Achieving just the right balance is often a matter of trial and error.

When stitching the individual pieces in this chapter, I tried to mix and blend colors in unusual ways. In the *Tiger* rug, I used four different shades of yellow and three of orange, mixing them endlessly. I would thread the needle with three shades of yellow wool and one of orange, for example, and work on a section; then, after rethreading the needle with, say, two shades of orange and two yellow strands, I would move to another section. For the black markings, I created many different shades of black by mixing the wool with strands of brown, purple, and gray. In the *Two Fish* pillow, an unanticipated dimension was added when I threaded two different shades of green through the needle and, as I turned the canvas to stitch the design, the wool twisted, exposing the different shades of green. This kind of color-mixing creates the effect of fading that gives the piece depth as well as the look of genuine old textiles. It also keeps the eye moving around the piece, which gives it a sense of movement.

I am most attracted to the patterns of ancient cultures. The Ghana chessboard and the Mola slippers are examples, because I think their abstract forms allow for greater individual freedom of expression and variation. It is ironic that the most primitive designs can, at times, provide such wonderful inspiration for contemporary designs.

Biblical animals march around the frame of this abstract representation of Noah's Ark. Using only black and white created a minimalist effect.

Above: The red evening bag displays one of the many ways that needlepoint can be used. The free-form designs were stitched with heavy shimmering cotton thread and narrow rows of seed beads. Right: The varying colors and patterns of these bangles are reminiscent of vibrant Guatemalan designs.

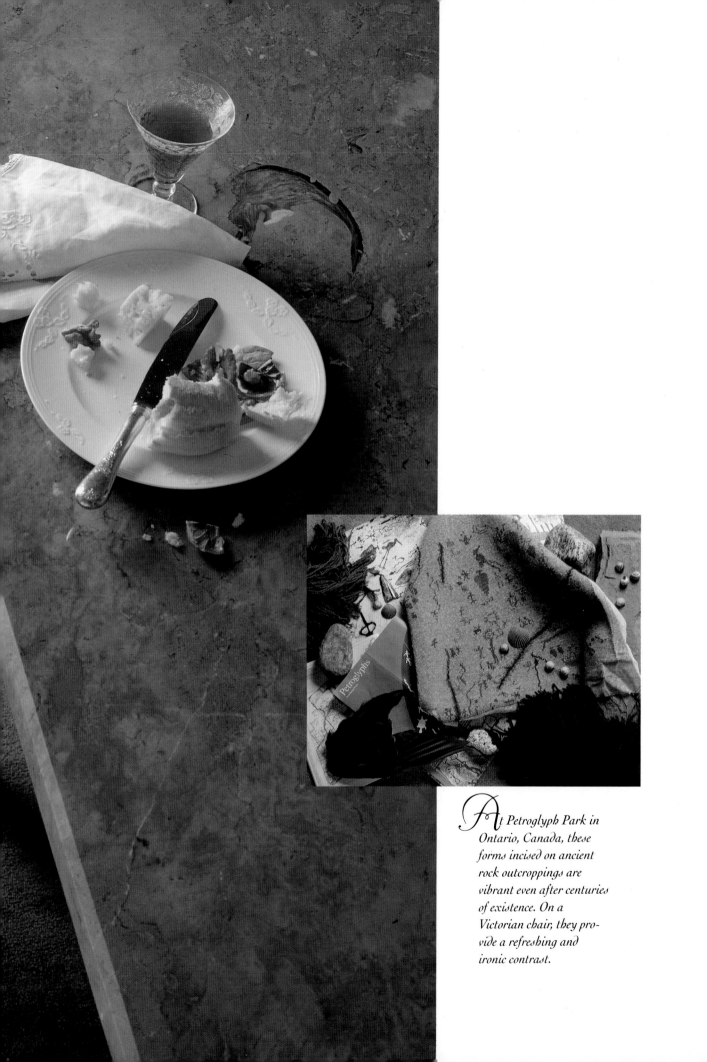

At Petroglyph Park in Ontario, Canada, these forms incised on ancient rock outcroppings are vibrant even after centuries of existence. On a Victorian chair, they provide a refreshing and ironic contrast.

Preceding pages: The "Rose" pillow lives comfortably in both traditional and contemporary settings, although it was originally made to complement an Oriental rug. The free-form shapes are stitched in three shades of rose, which I mixed and matched to obtain different effects. Right: Two by two, elephants, camels, turtles, zebras, and a menagerie of other animals march across the "Noah's Ark" pillow. Above: Detail of "Animal Stripes" pillow, shown behind "Noah's Ark" pillow.

*bove: The unusual Roman-temple style of this clock works well
with Biedermeier furniture. Right: On the "Boteh," or paisley, pillow,
many shades of dark and light colors were woven together to create the
sense of shadow and light found in Oriental rugs. The inspiration for
the zigzag footstool came from an Indian textile pattern.*

Left: The design for the "Papyrus Flowers" pillow was inspired by pictures of Egyptian tomb drawings that I found in a book called The Pleasures of Pattern. *To further the Egyptian theme, I used blue wool to represent the Nile River, and I added wild trim to jazz up the sedate flowers. Above: Three rug designs were combined to create the exotic patterns of the "Oriental" mirror. The hands that rise up on either side are like those found on ancient prayer rugs indicating to worshipers where to place their hands when praying to Allah. The universal symbols of the sun, moon, and stars overlook the mirror.*

The "Kazak" and "Pome-
granate" pillows are based
on old designs from
Oriental rugs. The design
in the center of the large
"Kazak" pillow is an
abstract tree of life, taken
from ancient prayer rugs.
The small "Kazak" pillow
shows off the bold forms
used by the nomadic Kazak
tribe. The pomegranate was
a symbol of fertility in the
Ottoman Empire.

Preceding pages: These pillow designs were taken directly from paintings by Dutch artist Piet Mondrian. In one of the paintings that I wished to needlepoint, Mondrian had turned his square canvas so that it became diamond shaped as it hung on the wall. I tried to create a similar effect by stitching the diamond and then adding the purple background. Above: Wonderfully stylized ice-fishing lures provided inspiration for the "Two Fish" pillow. Right: Art Deco is a wonderful source for needlepoint design ideas. This valence is not yet complete as it should extend the full length of the French doors.

Left: Purple gallinules, with their iridescent plumage, make great subjects for needlepoint. These odd birds do have red legs and beaks and purple-black bodies. Above: Mola designs by Panamanian Indians of South America inspired these exotic needlepointed slippers. The star in the center is a traditional Mola motif.

Appendix

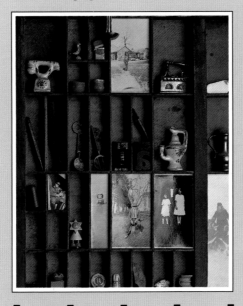

There are many excellent books that cover needlepoint technique in great detail. Instead of repeating that information here I will, instead, explain only materials and techniques that are particular to my designs.

MATERIALS

Canvas: The pieces featured in this book were made using a wide variety of canvas or mesh sizes—from a very coarse 7 mesh (7 stitches to the inch) for the *Tiger* rug (page 66) up to 18 mesh for the Ritz Hotel *Palm Court* portrait (page 23). Needlepoint canvas is available from 5 mesh to 24 mesh and the size you use will be determined by the design you have selected as well as your personal preference. The higher mesh numbers mean more stitches per square inch—12 mesh has 144 stitches per square inch, for example. Therefore, when you wish to have a lot of detail you should probably choose from 12 to 24 mesh; conversely, for a needlepoint rug you would use 5 or 7 mesh canvas. Remember that any of the designs in this book can be stitched on a larger or smaller mesh canvas for a very different look. This is discussed further under "Design." I have used Zweigart™ single interlock canvas for all of my pieces, and I believe it is the best available. If you are not able to buy Zweigart™ canvas at your local needlework shop you can order it from the mail-order suppliers listed under "Suppliers" at the end of this section.

Needles: You should always use a tapestry needle when you work in needlepoint. A tapestry needle has a blunt end that slips easily between the threads of the canvas. A size 18 needle is appropriate for 10 to 14 mesh canvas. Size 5 or 7 mesh canvas will require a larger needle and 18 mesh will require a finer needle.

Yarn: For strength, durability, and its beautiful luster, Persian tapestry wool is unrivaled. My favorite is sold under the brand name Paternayan™ and comes in a range of 405 colors. I have worked successfully with other wools, but Paternayan™ is my wool of choice (see list at end of this section for supplier information). All of my designs call for Paternayan™ wool with the exception of the *Medieval Bunny* design (page 24), which uses Anchor™ tapestry wool. Should you wish to substitute another brand of wool, the salesperson at your local needlework shop will be able to help you convert the Paternayan™ wool colors to the corresponding colors of another brand. Paternayan™ wool comes in triple strands. For 10 mesh canvas use all three strands in your needle to form one stitching strand. For 12, 13, and 14 mesh use two of the three strands in your needle. For 18 and 24 mesh canvas use one strand, and for 5 or 7 mesh canvas you will need four strands. Since Persian tapestry wool comes in triple strands, which can be separated, it is very easy to broaden your color range by using two or more different colors simultaneously in your needle.

This is not to say that other materials cannot be used in needlepoint; in fact, I strongly encourage you to experiment, if not on your actual piece then on a scrap piece of canvas. I have experimented with two types of cotton embroidery floss—six-stranded and heavy single-stranded—and seed beads, and have been very pleased with the results. Metallic thread is a material I was initially skeptical about but have begun to use more. It can be bold and exciting when used alone or subtle when mixed with wool. The only drawback to working with metallic thread is that it tends to fray quickly, so you should use shorter lengths than you would of Persian wool. Although it is expensive, silk thread is a superb material for needlepoint. Silk can be used in small sections as a highlight or accent because, having a very reflective surface patina, it contrasts strongly with the softer luster of wool. In short, almost anything that can be threaded into a needle can be used in needlepoint. In the future I plan to experiment with sequins, larger beads, and even feathers. Feel free to try any materials, however un-orthodox they may seem, to reach your artistic goals.

TECHNIQUES

Stitching: I have stitched all of my designs using the half-cross stitch. It works up very quickly and uses thirty percent less wool than either the basketweave or continental stitches. I work without using a frame because the needlepoint remains easy to carry—I can stuff a large pillow canvas with extra wool into my handbag and work anywhere. Also, the needlepoint design can be worked up more quickly because you can use a continuous sewing motion instead of the two motions—up and down—needed when using a frame. Although the frame does prevent much of the distortion that occurs when you do not use one, it only takes a little time to block a piece to bring it back into shape.

I generally begin a project by stitching all of the details of a design and then filling in the background. This way, stitches can be added easily later on or, if necessary, the background color can be used to conceal errors. Needle-point is a very forgiving medium, so you needn't worry if you leave out or add an unexpected extra stitch.

Color: What distinguishes superb needlepoint from the mundane is imaginative use of color. I use two strands of very close shades of the same color in my needle wherever possible because even that very subtle variation can make a piece look much richer. The human eye perceives an area of solid color as flat. But when two or more close tones of color are mixed, that area becomes alive and vibrant. If you look closely at my Oriental rug pieces (page 85) you will see that there are no areas of flat color. Each part of the design is punctuated with lines and individual stitches in variant shades of the same color. Sometimes this means going back over an area several times with differing tones of one color. This is also how I work the foliage in the house portraits, selecting four or five shades of green and stitching them in random spots over a given area until it becomes completely filled with dappled color.

House Portraits: To create a house portrait, take a photograph of the front facade of the house straight on (it is much more difficult to work from an angled view). From that photograph, draw a picture that incorporates all the features you wish to portray. This drawing should be rendered in the size the portrait is to be; most of my portraits measure eight inches by ten inches. Then transfer the outlines from the drawing onto your canvas; 12 or 13 mesh should give enough detail. Begin with the windows, doors, and other details; then complete the roof and walls. Once the house is completed, fill in the foliage, lawn, trees, and flowers. The sky should be the last part of

Left: This snapshot shows the "Robb House," once a Victorian hunting lodge, and now a private residence. Above: Replicating the brick-and-flintwork construction required a good deal of complex stitching.

the portrait filled in. The outlines on the canvas serve as my guide for the shape of the house and its details, but for the coloring and shading I refer directly to the photograph. To practice, you can make a miniature version of the house portrait (say, four inches by five inches) in which everything is the same size as it is in your photograph. This will help you work out the proportions and foliage placement and will take a fraction of the time that a full portrait requires. I generally frame my house portraits, but they can also be made into charming pillows or footstools.

Blocking: Once your piece is stitched it should be blocked to bring all the stitches back into proper alignment. Roll the needlepoint into a dampened towel. The towel should only be damp, not soaking wet, and the best towel to use is a white linen tea-towel. If your towel is colored be absolutely certain that it will not run or bleed onto your needlepoint. Leave the needlepoint rolled in the towel for four to six hours or until the canvas becomes damp and pliable. To be sure that you block the piece squarely, draw its correct shape and exact dimensions on a piece of plywood (or hardwood) large enough for the needlepoint plus two inches on all sides, or on a piece of paper (using only a waterproof pen) that you attach to the plywood. Stretch the needlepoint and block it by nailing it face down onto the wood: begin at the corners and put nails in at ¾-inch intervals around the entire perimeter of the piece. Leave it to dry thoroughly for at least a few days. If the piece is particularly distorted, apply a thin layer of wallpaper paste to the back of the needlepoint immediately after it has been blocked and is still damp. Remember to check that the contents of the paste won't damage the fibers by testing it on a small piece of the needlepoint or on a few of the wool fibers. Simply apply some of the paste, allow to dry, and observe the results. Once the needlepoint has dried, the nails can be removed and your piece can be made up.

Finishing Touches: Special finishing touches can add an extra flourish or an element of surprise to needlepoint. If your piece is to be framed, consider trying something out of the ordinary—choose an Old Master type gilded frame as I did for my *Goose with the Golden Egg* (page 26), or attach unlikely items to the frame, as with my *Noah's Ark in Black and White* (page 70) and *Wheatfields* mirror (page 44). A deep-colored mat can highlight a particular color in your piece, or a thin border of marbleized paper can add elegance. For needlepoint pillows I am particularly fond of using rope braid and other types of trimming. My *Papyrus Flowers* pillow (page 82) sports a wonderful thick pink fringe trim and the *Angel* pincushion (page 52) has a border of shiny gold coins.

The shape of your needlepoint piece doesn't necessarily have to conform to its unfinished outlines. By appliquéing pieces of cloth such as a printed velvet or damask around the needlepoint, you can completely change its look and shape. I did just that with the *American Flag* tea cozy (page 47) and the *Canada Flag* egg cozy (page 46)—the denim background and appliquéd stars, eagle, and crown all became important elements of these gently humorous pieces. It is important to keep an open mind. What might seem an unlikely idea at first could actually be the seed of an ingenious finishing touch.

Working from Our Charts: Every stitch in a needlepoint design is represented on a chart as a tiny colored square or box, hence the name "box chart." Although you can begin to work anywhere in a chart, I find it easiest to begin with the bottom line because it serves as a good reference point for completing the rest of the design. You should be aware that the colors used in the charts that follow are not always exact reproductions of the original colors: sometimes they must be altered to make a chart easier to follow, especially in cases where the colors are very close in tone. However, the wool color numbers are the same as those that I used in the pieces in the photographs in this book. For all charts, unless otherwise indicated, the wool color numbers are for Paternayan™ wool. In addition, all the wool amounts given here are only approximate and have been estimated for the half-cross stitch. Should you use the basketweave or continental stitch you will need thirty percent more of each color. It is always preferable to buy extra wool if you have any doubts about how much you will need.

Personalizing a Chart: Think of a chart as a needlepoint road map from which you can deviate as much as you like. In fact, an excellent way to begin the process of learning how to design your own needlepoint creations is to take a chart and alter it to suit your fancy. Changing the background color will instantly change the look of a design (always stitch a section of the pattern and then fill in just a small area with the new background color to be sure that you like your idea). Changing one or more colors within the design pattern can create a subtler effect. Another alternative is to stitch a design on a larger canvas mesh size than the one suggested—10 mesh instead of 12 mesh, for example. Your finished piece will be larger and the pattern will be bolder. Conversely, make up a design in a smaller size mesh—14 mesh instead of 12 or 10 mesh—for a smaller, more detailed piece. Another effective way to use the charted designs is by combining elements from two or more charts, using the central motif from one chart with the border of another. Another option is to use a small portion of a charted pillow design to create other items. Any of the border designs in this book would make a beautiful belt, pair of suspenders, or camera strap. You could also use one section of a design to make a purse-size makeup bag or eyeglass case. The possibilities are endless.

To make a chart easier to follow, trace the outlines from the chart design onto your canvas using a waterproof pen (ink that is not waterproof could seep through your stitches and spoil the wool colors). Treat the canvas as if it were a piece of tracing paper and place it over the design. Wherever possible, trace the design along the actual lines of the canvas so that it is clear exactly where the outlines begin and end. Either fill in the areas of color by eye, as I do, or paint them in with a water-based acrylic paint. If you use paint, apply it lightly to avoid clogging the holes of the canvas.

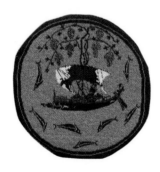

QUIMPER

Design from contents page

Finished dimensions: 14 × 14 inches

Canvas/Mesh size: 12 stitches per inch

Color number	Wool amounts
261	170 yards
726	25 yards
611	20 yards
832	18 yards
540	14 yards
541	10 yards
610	4 yards
221	3 yards

NOAH'S ARK

Design from page 79

Finished dimensions: 18½ × 18½ inches

Canvas/Mesh size: 12 stitches per inch

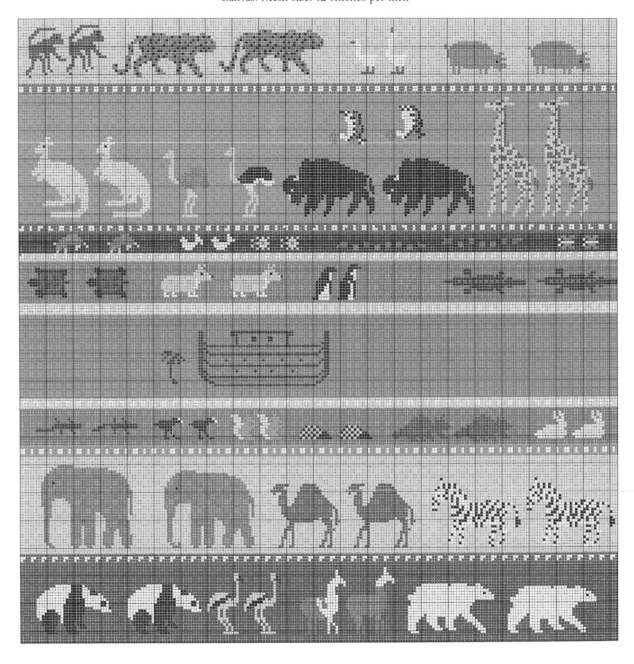

Color number		Wool amounts	Color number		Wool amounts
	512	70 yards		260	33 yards
	314	68 yards		510	31 yards
	561	66 yards		320	27 yards
	324	52 yards		200	23 yards
	560	50 yards		564	17 yards
	321	41 yards		313	13 yards
	322	38 yards		312	12 yards

MEDIEVAL BUNNY

Design from page 24

Finished dimensions: 15 × 15 inches

Canvas/Mesh size: 12 stitches per inch

Anchor Color number		Wool amounts	Anchor Color number		Wool amounts
	850	157 yards		848	17 yards
	347	38 yards		144	17 yards
	217	27 yards		860	17 yards
	264	27 yards		340	17 yards
	570	27 yards		427	17 yards

Please note that Anchor tapestry wool is used for this piece.

ORVIETO

Design from pages 32 and 33
Finished dimensions: 15½ × 15½ inches
Canvas/Mesh size: 12 stitches per inch

Color number		Wool amounts
	260	118 yards
	540	77 yards
	541	28 yards
	771	23 yards
	350	13 yards
	772	5 yards

HEART IN HAND

Design from page 41

Finished dimensions: 15 × 15 inches

Canvas/Mesh size: 10 stitches per inch

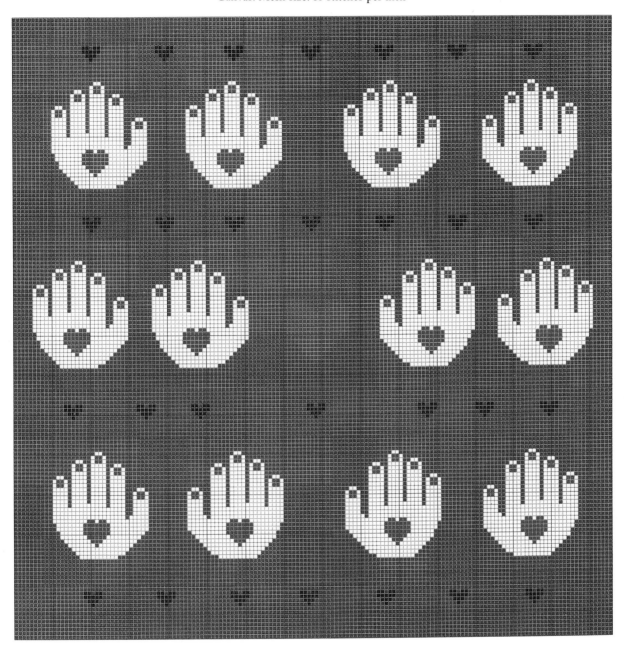

Color number		Wool amounts
■	520	116 yards
■	521	100 yards
□	262	53 yards
■	968	18 yards
■	910	13 yards

Please note: You should mix 520 and 521 to achieve a heathery green background. Use two strands of 521 with one strand of 520 and vice versa, alternating the color mix by row. For the little green hearts use only 520.

PENDLETON

Design from page 42

Finished dimensions: 11½ × 9¾ × 1¾ inches

Canvas/Mesh size: 10 stitches per inch

Color number		Wool amounts
	862	54 yards
	640	45 yards
	641	45 yards
	470	19 yards
	421	17 yards
	643	10 yards
	480	7 yards
	481	7 yards
	864	3 yards

Please note: use one strand each of 640 and 641 in the same needle for the
dark olive green. Do the same for the medium brown by using one strand each
of 480 and 481.

COUNTRY ANIMALS

Design from page 51

Finished dimensions: 15 × 15 inches

Canvas/Mesh size: 12 stitches per inch

Color number		Wool amounts
▓	969	195 yards
░	260	40 yards
█	220	21 yards

WATERMELON

Design from page 54

Finished dimensions: 3½ × 6½ inches

Canvas/Mesh size: 14 stitches per inch

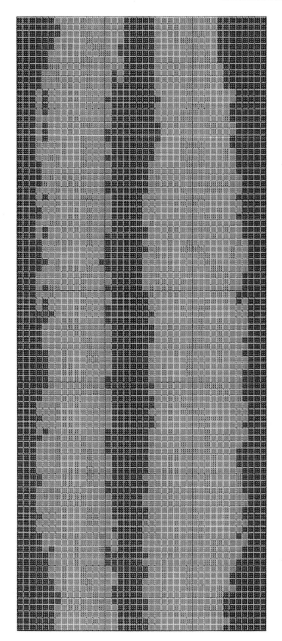 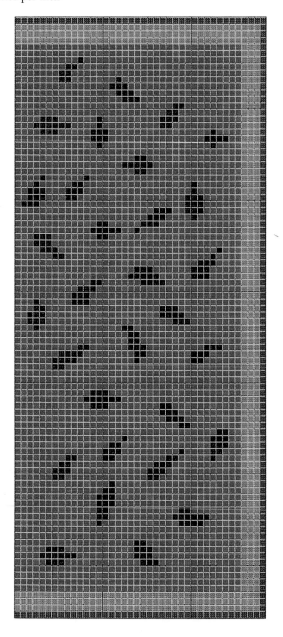

Color number		Wool amounts
	603	22 yards
	520	13 yards
	940	9 yards
	643	4 yards
	220	3 yards
	950	3 yards

NAVAJO

Design from page 56

Finished dimensions: 6½ × 9 inches

Canvas/Mesh size: 13 stitches per inch

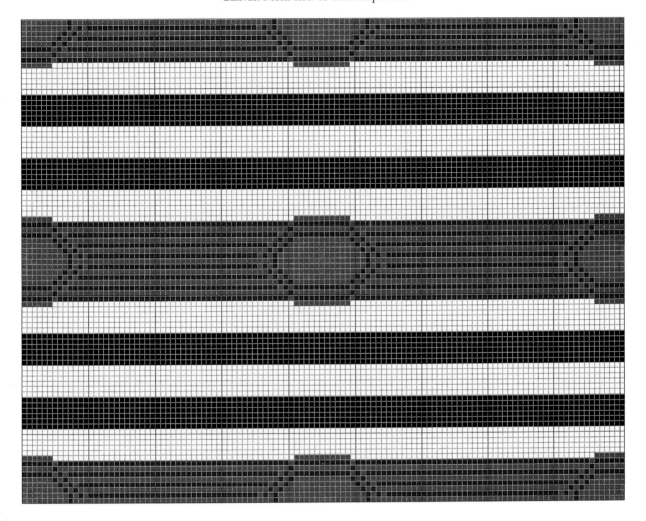

Color number		Wool amounts
☐	756	16 yards
■	221	14 yards
■	930	7 yards
■	571	5 yards
■	543	4 yards

HUMMINGBIRDS

Design from page 61

Finished dimensions: 15 × 15 inches

Canvas/Mesh size: 12 stitches per inch

Color number	Wool amounts	Color number	Wool amounts
546	138 yards	969	9 yards
630	27 yards	210	9 yards
632	17 yards	221	5 yards
610	15 yards	260	4 yards
971	10 yards	540	4 yards

PAPYRUS FLOWERS

Design from page 82

Finished dimensions: 9½ × 9¼ inches

Canvas/Mesh size: 12 stitches per inch

Color number		*Wool amounts*		*Color number*		*Wool amounts*
	571	17 yards			591	9 yards
	580	17 yards			592	9 yards
	520	16 yards			945	5 yards
	261	11 yards			696	3 yards
	610	7 yards				

Please note: use one strand each of 571 and 580 in the same needle for the aqua
blue, and one strand each of 591 and 592 in the same needle for the deep blue.

HEART CHRISTMAS ORNAMENT

Design from page 62

Finished dimensions: 3½ × 4 inches

Canvas/Mesh size: 14 stitches per inch

Color number		Wool amounts
■	661	6 yards
■	968	5 yards
□	261	4 yards

DALMATIAN CHRISTMAS ORNAMENT

Design from page 62

Finished dimensions: 5 × 4½ inches

Canvas/Mesh size: 14 stitches per inch

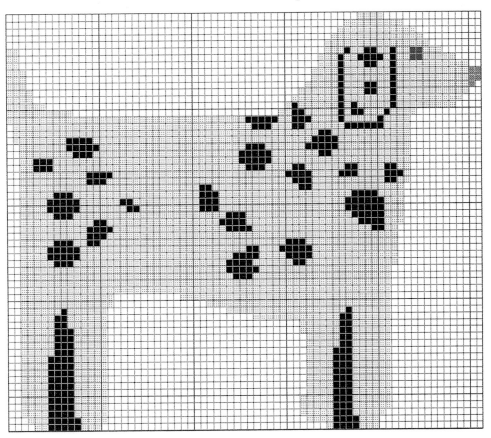

Color number		Wool amounts
	263	10 yards
	220	4 yards
	542	1 yard
	354	1 yard

DIAMOND CHRISTMAS ORNAMENT

Design from page 62

Finished dimensions: 2¾ × 2¾ inches

Canvas/Mesh size: 14 stitches per inch

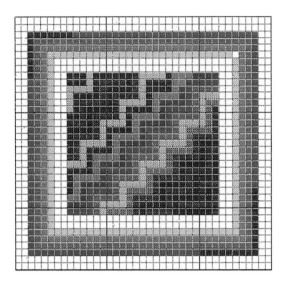

Color number		Wool amounts
☐	260	3 yards
▨	841	1 yard
▨	821	1 yard
▨	771	1 yard
▨	934	1 yard
▨	352	1 yard
▨	353	1 yard
▨	311	1 yard
▨	331	1 yard
▨	332	1 yard
▨	321	1 yard

PINEAPPLE CHRISTMAS ORNAMENT

Design from page 62

Finished dimensions: 5½ × 4¼ inches

Canvas/Mesh size: 14 stitches per inch

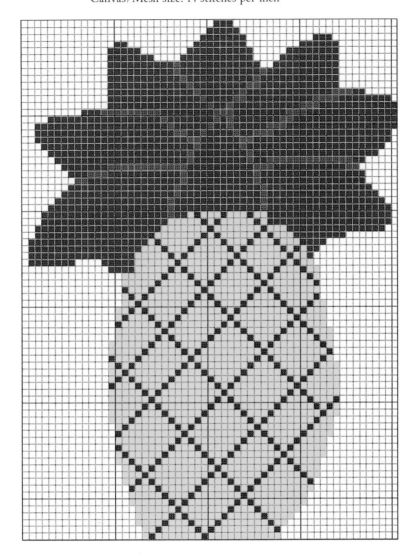

Color number		Wool amounts
■	660	8 yards
□	726	8 yards
■	470	5 yards
■	692	2 yards

Please note: to make the six pointed stars, use one strand of 470 and overstitch
them onto the yellow background of each diamond.

POMEGRANATE

Design from page 84

Finished dimensions: 8 × 8 inches

Canvas/Mesh size: 13 stitches per inch

	Color number	Wool amounts
	263	38 yards
	571	11 yards
	840	9 yards
	726	7 yards
	500	4 yards
	950	4 yards
	520	3 yards

SMALL KAZAK

Design from page 85

Finished dimensions: 15 × 15 inches Canvas/Mesh size: 13 stitches per inch

Color number	Wool amounts	Color number	Wool amounts
263	50 yards	950	3 yards
221	40 yards	571	3 yards
901	33 yards	421	3 yards
530	30 yards	743	3 yards
727	25 yards	734	3 yards
968	23 yards	726	2 yards
520	23 yards	521	2 yards
570	10 yards	460	2 yards
570*	4 yards	441	2 yards
571*	4 yards	733	2 yards
500	3 yards	534	1 yard

*Please note: Use one strand of 570 and one strand of 571, 4 yards of each, in your needle to make this color.

MONDRIAN II

Design from pages 86 and 87
Finished dimensions: 11½ × 11½ inches
Canvas/Mesh size: 12 stitches per inch

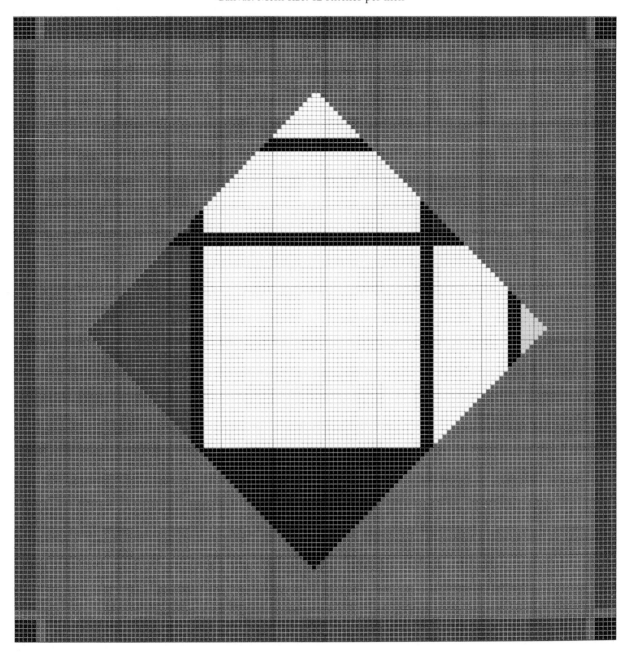

Color number		*Wool amounts*
	341	79 yards
	260	27 yards
	680	18 yards
	220	10 yards
	940	4 yards
	712	3 yards
	540	1 yard

PURPLE GALLINULES

Design from page 90

Finished dimensions: 15 × 15 inches

Canvas/Mesh size: 10 stitches per inch

Color number		Wool amounts
	715	142 yards
	713	40 yards
	712	20 yards
	220	14 yards
	221	9 yards
	950	6 yards
	260	4 yards
	968	2 yards

Suppliers

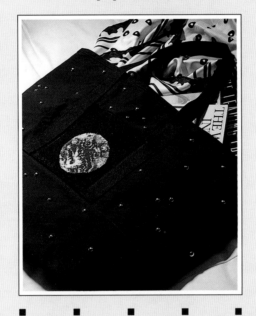

■ ■ ■ ■ ■

Zweigart® Needlepoint Canvas

If Zweigart® canvas is not available at your local needle-work shop it can be ordered by mail from the following suppliers:

UNITED STATES

THE WORLD IN STITCHES
298 Great Road
Littleton, Massachusetts 01460
Telephone: (508) 486-8330

ROSE GARDEN NEEDLEWORK & CRAFTS
P.O. Box 261
Madison, Tennessee 37115
Telephone: (800) 826-1998

MARY MAXIM
2001 Holland Avenue
Port Huron, Michigan 48061
Telephone: (313) 987-2000

CANADA

GISELE'S HOUSE OF NEEDLECRAFT
1276 Wellington Street
Ottawa, Ontario K1Y 3A7
Telephone: (613) 728-3114

VILLAGE STITCHERY LTD.
150-8380 Lansdowne Road
Richmond, British Columbia
Telephone: (604) 278-3666

UNITED KINGDOM

DUNLICRAFT LTD.
Pullman Road
Wigston
Leicester, LE8 2DY
Telephone: (0533) 811040

Paternayan™ Persian Tapestry Wool

Almost any fine needlework shop will carry this wool. It is
distributed by:

JOHNSON CREATIVE ARTS
445 Main Street
West Townsend, Massachusetts 01474
Telephone: (508) 597-8794

UNITED STATES

KELSEA SALES
151 Nashdene Road, Unit 8
Scarborough, Ontario, M1V 2T3
Telephone: (416) 298-0443
Call or write for the name of your nearest local shop.

CANADA

M. P. STONEHOUSE LTD.
Albion Mills
Wakefield, Yorkshire WF2 9SG
Telephone: (0924) 373456
Call or write for the name of your nearest local shop.

UNITED KINGDOM

Needlepoint kits of selected designs by Catherine Reurs are
available. For further information, you may write or call:

CATHERINE REURS NEEDLEPOINT
186 Rowayton Avenue
Rowayton, Connecticut 06853
Telephone: (203) 838-8761

Acknowledgments

So many wonderful friends, old and new, have helped me stitch together this book. It was no small task, and I would like to express my heartfelt thanks to everyone involved.

I am most grateful to Andy Stewart and Leslie Stoker for believing that needlepoint is art and for giving me the privilege of publishing with Stewart, Tabori & Chang. To my editor, Andrea Danese, I extend my warmest thanks for her help and enthusiastic support throughout the project. My deep appreciation goes to Lynn Pieroni for her elegant design, and to everyone else at Stewart, Tabori & Chang, whose efforts result in such superb books, it has been a great pleasure working with all of you.

This book would not have been possible without the artistic talent and commitment of photographer, Richard Desmarais, his assistant, David Radburn, and stylist, Ursula Kaiser. Their combined artistic vision, experience, and resourcefulness assured the fine photography and beautiful setups which make my needlepoint pieces come alive. I would like to thank Jill Herbers, who distilled our many hours of conversation into the text of this book.

My husband, Jiri Stanislav, allowed me to focus my energy on this book, and he was always behind the project one hundred percent.

My mother and stepfather, MaryAnn and Ray Parker, and my sister, Jill Reurs, were also most supportive. Marie and Fitz Fitzpatrick, who have been extended family for as long as I can remember, gave so generously of their time and hospitality during my many trips to New York City. They always gave me a home away from home.

My dear friends Belinda Coote and Dennis and Melissa Foreman were a constant source of encouragement and ideas for new pieces. A very special thank you to Russ de Burlo, who believed in my work as much as I did, and without whose support I might not have survived that first year after leaving the bank. I also wish to thank Lynette Bisnath for all her support during the initial stages of the development of this book.

My friends and clients very kindly allowed me to borrow my pieces back for the photography. I am grateful to: Richard and Sylvie Bauer, Hugh Ehrman, Ron and Mavis Elstone, Thomas and Judith Fisher, Michael Franke, Linda Freshwater, Mrs. Sheila Garfield, Mrs. Joan Golfar, John, Izzy and Edward Harrap, Mr. Terry Holmes, Richard McLaughlin, Mrs. Jane Robb, Isabella Rossellini, Sue Shaw, Richard and Louise Walker, Katrina Williams, Luke Wilson, Mr. and Mrs. Robert Winter, Peter Vani, and Max von Geier.

So many people generously allowed us to borrow props or use their locations for our photography. I would like to thank Angelika Abbott, Bev and Ron Baxter Smith, Jackie and Paul Browning, Pat and Jim Bullock, Kathleen Cannon, Dee Chenier of D. Chenier & Associates, Inc., Dakota Jackson of Dakota Jackson, Inc., Don Ellis, Larry and Anstace Esmonde-White, Joussef Hasbani of L'Atelier, Karen Gray and Paul Crouch, Evelyn Jardim of La Loggia, Don Johnson, Vi Jull of French Country Antiques, Kim Lewis, Greg Kay of Willow Art, Patricia Hanson of Klaus Nienkamper, Mrs. T.A. Peake, Richard and Hilda Reuter, Dino Ricci and Sandra Bezic Ricci, Taylor & Browning Design Associates, Joanne Thring and Rita Tsantis of Filligree Linens & Lace, Phillip Van Leeuwen, and Cynthia Wise of Wise Kalan & Associates.

When time was of the essence I could always count on Shirley Hernandez, Linda Terrill, Gem Angel, and Nora Maltby to help me assemble or finish stitching pieces for the book. Their nimble fingers made all the difference in meeting our deadlines.

Prop Credits

Cover: furniture, props, and location courtesy of Florence Dampierre of Dampierre and Company, 79 Greene Street, New York, New York 10012.

Back cover: props courtesy of French Country Antiques, 160 Pears Avenue, Toronto, Ontario M5R 1T2.

Title page: furniture and props courtesy of Wise Kalan & Associates, Inc., 160 Pears Avenue, Toronto, Ontario M5R 1T2.

Contents page: props courtesy of French Country Antiques.

page 24: teak bench from L'Atelier, 1228 Young Street, Toronto, Ontario M4T 1W3. Photographed in Allan Gardens, 160 Gerrard Street, East, Toronto, Ontario.

pages 34 and 35: props courtesy of Van Leeuwen Boomcamp, Ottawa (see Phillip Van Leeuwen for address).

page 40: props courtesy of La Loggia, 160 Pears Avenue, Toronto, Ontario M5R 1T2.

page 44: props courtesy of La Loggia.

page 55: props courtesy of La Loggia and French Country Antiques.

page 56: miniature willow furniture made by Greg Kay of Willow Art, 238 Montrose Avenue, Toronto, Ontario M6G 3G7.

page 58: twig furniture, Pendleton blanket, floor rug, and most small props from Don Ellis of Don Ellis-Antiques, RR-3, Dundas, Ontario L9H 5E3.

page 59: props courtesy of French Country Antiques.

page 61: photographed in Allan Gardens.

page 65: furniture and props courtesy of Phillip Van Leeuwen, 430 Hazeldean Road, Kanata, Ontario K2L 1T9.

page 67: stool base and props courtesy of Dakota Jackson, Inc., 306 East 61st Street, New York, New York 10021.

page 70: twig table courtesy of Don Ellis.

page 72: floral boxes courtesy of Filigree Linens and Lace, 1210 Young Street, Toronto, Ontario M4T 1W1.

page 79: bed linen courtesy of Filigree Linens and Lace.

page 80: desk and props courtesy of Wise Kalan & Associates, Inc.

page 85: furniture and props courtesy of Klaus Nienkamper, 300 King Street, East, Toronto, Ontario M5A 1K4.

pages 86 and 87: furniture and props courtesy of Phillip Van Leeuwen.

page 89: chair courtesy of Taylor & Browning Design Associates, 10 Price Street, Toronto, Ontario M4W 1Z4.

page 90: photographed at Larry and Anstace Esmonde-White's 'The Country Garden,' RR-5, Kemptville, Ontario K0G 1J0.

In **S** *plendid Detail*

Design by Lynn Pieroni

Composed in Bembo and Cochin by
Trufont Typographers, Inc.,
Hicksville, New York

Printed and bound by
Tien Wah Press (Pte), Ltd.,
Singapore